PRAYERS
OF AGREEMENT
FOR WIVES

Amanda R. Moody

Scripture quotations, unless noted otherwise, are taken from the Holy Bible.

Cover photo by Jaime Renville
www.jaimemariephotography.blogspot.com

Author's photo by Amanda Reed
http://www.amandascreativemoments.net/

CONTENTS

ACKNOWLEDGMENTS

I thank God for sending His son, Jesus, to redeem us and set us free. I'm so thankful to be a vessel He works through to pray His will for marriages. Without Him I can do nothing. I pray this book causes Him to be glorified and brings forth His kingdom and His will in the earth.

I thank my husband, Rob. You were the first to show me the love of God and lead me to Him. Thank you for allowing God to work through you to love me and teach me. Thank you for always reminding me to keep my eyes on God and what He's called me to do. Thank you for your prayers and your patience as God works in me. You are an excellent husband and I am blessed to be your wife. I look forward to spending the rest of our days walking together as one.

To my daughters, Gabrielle, Lauren, Charity, and Grace, thank you for being a blessing. Thank you for being so patient during the many early mornings, late nights, and hours in worship and prayer. God teaches me so much through my relationships with you. You are beautiful, virtuous, mighty daughters of the Most-High God and I look forward to everything He plans to accomplish in and through you.

To my Pastors Mark and Linda Cowart, thank you for lifting the standard and pulling on Church For All Nations to arise and operate as the body of Christ. You provoked me to "do something" with the ideas and gifts God placed in me.

To my Pastors Charles and Angelique Price in Okinawa, Japan, thank you for developing the gifts of God within me and challenging me to study to show myself approved unto God. Your effort, prayers, and inspiring words pushed me further into the will of God.

To MomMoody (Stephanie Moody), thank you for always seeing me through the Father's eyes. Your example continues to teach me the power of prayer and how to access the heart of the Father. Thank you for your love and tireless intercession on my behalf.

To Dorothea Mapp and my mom (Theresa Surley), thank you for contributing your time and talent to review and polish this book.

To all my sisters and brothers in Christ, thank you for your example, love, encouragement, and prayers. I pray you come to know the impact you have in God's kingdom. It is my prayer that the world sees the Father through His sons and daughters.

PREFACE

This began in 2005 with a small group of wives joined together to agree in prayer for their marriages. It soon grew to over 150 wives petitioning heaven in agreement for 30 days. The testimonies quickly began to roll in. Before we even reached day 15, two husbands had rededicated their lives to Christ. Many more wives reported breakthroughs in their marriages throughout and even beyond our 30 days of prayer. By the end we found we were stronger wives with more faith and confidence in God and His word.

It is not a requirement to pray these prayers as a group. A wife can certainly pray for her husband by herself and God's word will still manifest. I've just found that it is much easier when there are two or more people in agreement, standing in faith together, holding each other accountable, and encouraging one another. It reminds us that we are not in this alone. It lessens the likelihood of us allowing the enemy to isolate us and deceive us into thinking our prayers don't make a difference. In a group, wives are able to edify one another in the area(s) in which they have overcome. The wives have an opportunity to minister to one another with their God-given gifts. Together we are stronger than we are individually. I encourage every woman reading this book to get at least one sister in Christ to pray with. You don't have to meet everyday face to face; be led by the Holy Spirit. He knows what each of us needs and what will work in our lives. The important thing is that the wives are praying the Word of God in agreement for their own marriage and for the marriages of the women they're praying with. Also that each wife is encouraging others and being encouraged to pray, believe, and receive.

I pray every wife understands how powerful her prayers are. They aren't just nice things to say or hope for. Her prayers open the door for God to work in her life and in her marriage. Nothing can match the power of sowing the Word of God into her marriage. I pray she studies the Word and sows it into her heart until that is all that exists there. I pray she recognizes, becomes empowered in, and speaks with the authority God gave her to build, restore, and elevate her marriage. I pray she stands on the Word and expects manifestation knowing that God's word does not return null and void. Our prayers are seeds sown. We are not required to understand how the seeds bring forth fruit. We are only required to have faith in God. God is moved by our faith in Him.

For everyone who prays these prayers, I expect a harvest of reconciliation, a harvest of miracles, a harvest overflowing above all you could ever ask or think, and a harvest in this season.

May you know Him more today than ever before.

INTRODUCTION

You often hear people say, "There's power in numbers." This usually refers to the physical strength and influence that arises when people join themselves together for a common purpose. The spiritual side to "power in numbers" is much more significant and can produce a far more miraculous result. In Matthew 18:19-20, Jesus taught that if two agree on earth concerning anything that they ask, it will be done for them by the Father in heaven. For where two or three are gathered together in the name of Jesus, He is there in the midst of them. Jesus established a principle that when Christians agree in prayer, God will do what they've asked.

You may also hear people talk about how the world is suffering because men aren't fulfilling their roles as husbands and/or fathers. How they're treating women worse and becoming absentee and even unknown fathers. The more we hear this, the more we tend to accept it whether we like it or not. We may even find ourselves complaining too. If we are looking to change things, we are going about it all wrong. It's time to stop complaining and blaming, feeling hopeless, and adding to the problem. We have the means to change things. We have access, through Jesus, to the creator of the universe who has all power and authority in heaven and earth. Not only are we able to pray to God on our own but when we join with other believers we have increased "power in numbers." After all, Jesus said two believers can agree on anything, ask God for it, and it will be done for them. In other words, two wives can agree that they want God's will to be done in their marriages and when they ask God for it, it is done! Many wives agree that they want a better marriage. They agree on things they'd like to see changed. The problem is some wives don't use that power of agreement to pray and do something to change things.

As wives, it is vital that we learn and operate in the purpose God designed for us. A wife has much more impact than she may realize. The wife is the special help made suitable for the husband. Her actions, prayers, beliefs, confessions, and faith can open the door for miracles to occur in her marriage, herself, and her husband. God gave us very specific blessings and authority. In order to receive the blessings and authority we must acknowledge them, believe they are for us, and operate in them. What happens for some wives is they unknowingly spend much of their life learning how to create an unsuccessful marriage. This type of wife has accepted that her marriage is never going to be what she once imagined it would. She's tried to fix everything herself and has likely given up and settled for a life that is much less than what she dreamed of as a child. Proverbs 14 says a wise woman builds her house but the foolish one tears it down with her own hands. It seems some wives tear down their house without even knowing it. On the other hand, some wives know their house is falling but they don't know what to do about it. This is why it is important to learn and operate in the purpose that God designed specifically for the wife.

The wife has power and authority in her prayers for her husband. Her authority is not over her husband; rather it is over the atmosphere and everything surrounding her marriage. When she recognizes and operates in this authority according to God's word, she can open the door for God to change her and her marriage. This creates an atmosphere that is highly likely to produce change in her husband.

These prayers are not to ask God to do anything new. God has already supplied everything we need in His word. The prayers access the power, the grace, and the authority that God has already given us. With the prayers we pull up and remove all the seeds sown in our marriage that were not of God. Then we sow God's word into existence in our marriage and it brings forth fruit in abundance. Finally, through prayer we declare His word over our marriage as the foundation and the ultimate authority in every area. Our prayers start what God has already finished in His word. HALLELUJAH!

It is important to always enter into God's presence with praise and thanksgiving. As we approach the throne, we acknowledge who He is and what He's capable of. He is the great I AM. He is Almighty God. Worship Him for who He is. Whoever comes to God must believe that He is and that He is a rewarder of them that diligently seek Him (Hebrews 11:6). With an accurate perception of who He is and what He is capable of, we should find it easier to pray and believe that He is able, willing, and faithful to do what we ask.

Once we acknowledge who He is, we should examine ourselves to ensure we aren't hindering our prayers from being answered. Here are three things that can hinder our prayers:

1. **Believing God is able but questioning whether He is willing**. The question "Is God willing?" is easily answered when we ask according to His word. His word and His will are the same. The key is to study His word and find out what His will is regarding husbands, wives, marriage, or whatever you are praying about. Then pray for His word (His will) to be performed in those areas and know that His answer is "Yes." God desires for His will to be accomplished in our lives and He knows what we need before we even ask. Not only is He able to answer our prayers, but He is also willing to perform His word when we ask in the name of Jesus and faithfully believe we receive.

2. **Praying with the wrong motives**. The "change my husband so he can be better for me and then our marriage will be perfect" syndrome. This is a prayer offered from a position of blame and offense and masking it as an attempt to "help" the husband. When we pray for the husband, our motive must be an unselfish one. We are not petitioning God to change the

husband for the benefit of the wife. We are specifically praying for God's will to manifest for His glory. Now will this most likely benefit the wife? Yes, but that cannot be her motive if she expects God to answer her prayers. It is a heart issue she must resolve first.

3. **Praying but not really believing it is done.** This is the wife that prays and *hopes* God will answer but she's uncertain. She says things like, "I prayed but my husband has his own will and I can't change that. All I can do is pray and hope for the best." Prayers are not a wish-list of what *may* happen someday. This wife prays but doubts that what she's prayed for has been done. In this case, she will be easily distracted when she doesn't "see" any change. She may not realize that the delay in manifestation could be because of her wavering faith. She may think her doubts are just internal and they aren't affecting anything other than the battlefield of her mind. However, Proverbs 23:7 says as a man thinks in his heart, so is he. Her beliefs inevitably incite her behavior. Doubt in a wife's heart will manifest in her conversation and in her actions. She will continue to treat and speak to her husband as he is presently instead of what she has prayed for him to be. This reveals her belief that she hasn't received what she prayed for. In Mark 11:23-24, Jesus taught that when we ask in his name, we must believe we've received and not doubt in our heart...then we will have what we asked for. We walk by faith and not by sight. When we ask God, we must know that His heavenly angels immediately hearken to the voice of His word. Though we may not "see" immediate impact, impact has been made. When we grasp this truth, it's easier to walk by faith and call things that are not as though they are. We are less discouraged by what we see because we know the things that are unseen are greater than the things that are seen. If you find yourself struggling with doubt, here are some ways to overcome.

8

*Water your prayers with confessions

Faith comes by hearing and hearing by the word of God (Romans 10:17). Your confessions will build your faith and become the thoughts and meditation of your heart. Your thoughts will become your beliefs and provoke your behavior. You'll know that not only is God's word true, but it also pertains to you.

*Ask God to help you believe

In Mark 9:23-24 when Jesus asked the man if he believed for his son's healing, he said, "I do believe but help me with my unbelief Lord." Jesus said, "If you can believe then all things are possible for you." You can do all things through Christ who strengthens you. Don't try to believe in your own ability. Trust Him. Even when you can't imagine how He's going to do it, He makes a way where there seems to be no way. Have faith in Him and not yourself.

*Don't focus on your doubt

The more you think about, talk about, and meditate on how and why you doubt, the more it seems impossible to overcome. Bad habits are broken by starting new habits, not by focusing on the bad habit. Focus on faith. Take every doubtful thought captive and make it obey God's word. Close the door to doubt by opening your mouth, identifying it as a lie, and stating the truth of God's word. Submit to God, resist the devil, and he will flee from you (James 4:7).

*Write down every breakthrough

It may not be the full manifestation of what you're believing for, but it is a beginning. When a water dam is compromised it doesn't begin with a huge burst of water. It starts with a small crack and trickle of water. Engineers know this is a serious matter because it predicts the inevitable. The force of all the water continues to press against the dam until it breaks though with a mighty roar. When you recognize partial manifestation of your prayers, praise God, write it down, and keep it before you to encourage yourself. Keep calling on His word to breakthrough with a mighty roar.

*Take inventory of your conversation

Does what you say to others equate to what you are believing God for? Do you pray for one thing and then say something totally different when speaking to others about the situation? What comes out of your mouth when you get frustrated? Jesus said it is not what we put in our mouth that defiles us but that which comes out (Matthew 15:11). Remember, God hears you when you're praying *and* when you're not praying. Your words have creative power. You speak and it is. At the very least it manifests in your beliefs. You must ensure your conversation isn't creating doubtful thoughts in your mind. You don't want to unknowingly work against yourself and then wonder why your faith isn't where it should be.

*Take inventory of the conversation of those around you

Your thought life is greatly impacted by what you hear. Family, friends, TV, songs, books, etc. can either provoke you to good works or plant seeds of doubt and disbelief. You may already have enough of your own thoughts to take captive. Don't allow others to present more thoughts that are contrary to God's word. Instead, surround yourself with mature believers that will speak a word in season to encourage you. Get resources that quicken you to wait on the Lord, to stand therefore, and to have faith in God.

*Do something!

Faith is tangible. Faith is the substance of things hoped for and the evidence of things not seen (Hebrews 11:1). Faith is substance and evidence. It's not some spooky thing that is only measured in the spirit realm. Faith without works is dead (James 2:17). Hebrews 4:2 says the word didn't profit them because it wasn't mixed with faith. Faith provokes action.

10

Faith causes you to be a doer of the word and not just a hearer. It is the doer of the word that shall be blessed in his deed (James 1:25). As a doer, our works are the evidence of our faith. James 2:18 says I'll show you my faith by my works. Show your faith, to God and your husband, by your works. Remember, the husband that does not obey the word is won over by the godly conduct of his wife (1 Peter 3:1).

patience

Day 1 Marriage

.., God, I exalt You. You are the Lord of all good things. You are the Creator, the Beginning and the End, the Almighty God, my Father, my Savior, my Lord, and my First Love. I come to You, in the name of Jesus, to ask that Your will be done in my marriage. I present my marriage, my husband and myself to You for examination. Help me totally surrender every area to You. Over the next 30 days, I ask You to reveal everything that has hindered us from being in Your perfect will. I pray this be a time of purification for my marriage where all iniquity is revealed and removed. Lord, sanctify us with the truth of Your word. Work through me to transform my marriage into what You predestined it to be. I ask for Your grace because I know I can't do this in my own ability or strength. Today I surrender my thoughts and ask for my mind to be renewed with Your word. I welcome Your will into my life and marriage. Thank You for giving us the authority to bind and loose according to Your word. In the name of Jesus I bind the enemy and destroy all the plans against my marriage. Whether they are old or new, I declare them fruitless. I declare no weapon formed against us shall prosper. I come against all the works of the flesh and call a cease to the cycle of destruction they've caused. I decree the enemy has no place in my marriage. I welcome the power of Your Holy Spirit to minister wisdom and understanding to us. Right now I come against every form of separation. Whether it is physical, mental, spiritual, or emotional, I say that division is now destroyed and I call us together on one accord. We are one just as You said the two shall be united firmly and be one flesh. I decree what You have joined together, no man shall separate. I ask for Your heavenly angels to lift us up, take charge over us, and keep us in all our ways. Father, help us be sensitive to You as You reveal, correct, and lead. Help

12

us be patient and humble as You prune us from everything that is not bearing good fruit. Lord, I thank You for allowing us to come boldly to Your throne to obtain mercy and grace to help us in this time of need. Thank You for giving us Your word as our sword of the Spirit. Thank You for giving us the name of Jesus at which every knee shall bow. Thank You for giving us Your Holy Spirit, power over all the enemy's power, and mighty weapons to pull down strongholds. These are the greatest assets I have and I will utilize them as You've instructed me to. Right now I cast down everything attempting to distract us from seeing the truth in our marriage and in our lives. I take all our thoughts captive and bring them to the obedience of Christ. Lord, I ask for clarity in our thoughts, our vision, and our understanding. Condition us to be led by You. Today I submit my marriage to You for cleansing so it may be a vessel set apart for You and fit for Your use. I am in agreement with these women of God and I stand in great expectation of the abundant harvest to come. I believe what we've asked for is done in the name of Jesus, Amen.

Confessions

I speak to mountains and command them to be removed and cast into the sea. I do not doubt in my heart that what I've prayed for has been granted to me. I'm confident that I've received it! (Mark 11:23-24)

My husband and I sow to the Spirit and we reap everlasting life. We do not grow weary in doing well. We reap in due season because we do not faint. (Galatians 6:8-9)

I am a doer of God's word and not just a hearer and therefore I am a wise woman. My house is built upon a rock. Neither the rain, nor the floods, nor the wind that beats upon my house can make it fall because it is founded upon a rock. (Matthew 7:24-25)

13

Day 2 Virtuous Wife

Father God, I come to You, in the name of Jesus, to pray for You to help me walk as the virtuous woman and wife You predestined me to be. I know it is the woman who fears the Lord that shall be praised. Lord, I reverently and worshipfully fear You. I love You with all my heart, soul, mind, and strength and I desire to please You. Thank You for Your mercy that has kept me from being consumed and Your compassion that never fails. Thank You for Your grace that empowers me to live as You called me to live. Today I present myself as a living sacrifice to You. Help me with the things that I know need to change. Reveal the things that I know not. I ask You to show me any sin in my life, especially in my marriage. I confess those sins to You right now. I repent for every time I was hateful, critical, resentful, disrespectful, and unforgiving. I relinquish my old mindset, nature, automatic reactions, and independent ideas. I receive the mind of Christ. I know when I confess my sins You are faithful and just to forgive me and cleanse me from all unrighteousness. I receive Your forgiveness right now and I refuse to look back or harbor guilt any longer. I am set free from these things. No matter how great or how awful I was yesterday, I am a better wife today because of You and tomorrow I will be even better. Lord, condition me to have more compassion for my husband. I declare I will no longer look to him for fulfillment or acceptance but rather I will seek You for those things. Only You can truly fulfill me and make me whole. Only You can show me my worth as Your daughter. I accept the truth that I cannot change my husband. Only You have the power to do that and I let go of my thoughts and determination to do it myself. Lord, train me to pray effectively for him with the right motives in my heart. Guard the door of my lips so I won't speak anything destructive. Help me take charge of my facial expressions and crucify my flesh daily so I won't do anything to work against what You have begun in us. When my flesh wants to give in and go off, I ask You to remind me of the prayers I've prayed. Condition me to obey and submit to You so my husband may be won over by my godly lifestyle. I accept my husband as the head of our home where You placed him. Train me to reverence and support him as he learns to operate excellently in this position. I ask for insight into Your vision for him. I desire to see my husband the way You see him and appreciate him in a brand new way. I believe You've begun a new work in my marriage and I thank You for starting with me. Today I declare my marriage is better because of You and tomorrow it will be even better. I am in agreement with these women of God and I believe what we've asked for is done in the name of Jesus, Amen.

Confessions

I am kind and tenderhearted to my husband. I forgive him as God forgave me. (Ephesians 4:32)
I submit myself to my husband as to the Lord. (Ephesians 5:22)
My husband loves me as he loves himself. I respect and reverence my husband. I notice him. I prefer him. I honor him. I esteem him. I love him. I admire him. (Ephesians 5: 33)
If any husband does not obey the word of God, we agree that he will be won by the godly lifestyle of his wife. That as he observes the pure and modest way she conducts herself, together with her reverence for him, he will see her heart and her value in the eyes of God. We declare he will become a husband that dwells with his wife according to knowledge and gives honor to her. He will acknowledge that they are heirs together of the grace of life and his prayers will not be hindered. (1 Peter 3:1-7)

Day 3 The Workplace

Father God, I come to You, in the name of Jesus, to pray that Your will be done in our workplaces. Help us sharpen our perspective and see the influence we have on the atmosphere and others. Reveal Your purpose in our work so we may continuously focus on it and not be distracted. I ask for godly wisdom to make decisions with integrity and confidence. Condition us to prioritize and use time wisely to focus more on things that have value in Your kingdom. I declare, from this day forward, my husband and I will heartily do all things as unto You. Help us grow in patience and insight to see others as You see them so we may have more compassion and know how to reach them. I know our labor has a great purpose and I do not take this assignment lightly. Help us glorify You in everything we do so others will see Your greatness and be provoked to glorify You. I decree my husband is lifted up in his workplace because he has a kingdom assignment. I declare other men seek him out for help as they see Your glory shine through him. Lord, thank You for giving my husband favor with all men. Thank You for every opportunity You set before us. Train us to do things without murmuring and complaining so that we may be blameless in the midst of this crooked and perverse generation. I decree by Your grace we have strength to persevere and overcome even when others have given up and decided to quit. Father, I ask You to send spiritual mentors to disciple us. Help us recognize those You've sent to help us. Lord, reveal any part of our work that is outside of Your will. Direct us back into Your will and light the path so brightly that we see clearly where to go. In the name of Jesus, I bind slothfulness, idleness, and the spirit of fear. I cast down every thought that provokes us to procrastinate and avoid responsibility. I know we are above only and never beneath so I decree we will no longer stand aside feeling helpless or disassociated while the enemy comes to steal, kill, and destroy. Lord, I submit to You, I resist the devil and I command all darkness to flee. From this day forward, we will no longer accept the oppression of fear or confusion because we know these do not come from You. I welcome the spirit of power, the spirit of love, and the spirit of a sound mind to abide in us. Father, I ask You to develop the gifts You've placed in us so they grow more and more useful to You every day. Lord, thank You for our co-workers. I decree my husband and I will let our light so shine before them that they will see our good works and glorify You. I know our labor tends to life. I declare our work is successful and it will produce an eternal impact for Your glory and Your kingdom. I am in agreement with these women of God and I believe what we've asked for is done in the name of Jesus, Amen.

Confessions

My husband and I are like trees planted by the streams of water which bring forth fruit in its season. The leaves will not wither and whatever we do will prosper. (Psalm 1:3)

The beauty of the Lord our God is upon my marriage. He establishes the work of our hands. (Psalm 90:17)

My husband and I are steadfast, unmovable, always abounding in the work of the Lord. We know our labor is not in vain in the Lord. (1 Corinthians 15:58)

My husband and I walk worthy of the Lord and we fully please Him. We are fruitful in every good work. We steadily increase in the knowledge of God. (Colossians 1:10)

Day 4 Finances

Father God, I come to You, in the name of Jesus, to pray Your will for our finances. I know Your blessing makes us rich and adds no sorrow with it. Those who seek You will not lack any good thing and no good thing will You withhold from those who walk uprightly. Lord, we seek You, we walk uprightly, and we put our expectation in You. You supply all our needs according to Your riches and glory so I cast down the thought that we have to be self-sufficient. It is You that gives us the power to get wealth. Father, help us access that power with the right motives in our hearts. Lord, I confess the sin of wasting money on things I didn't need while telling myself I couldn't live without them. The only one I can't live without is You. I repent and I will never put anything above You again. We will not be greedy and trouble our house with selfish desires. I cast down the idea that we have to hoard everything in order to increase our wealth. I welcome the spirit of liberty to set us free from that poverty mindset. I decree we will not make the same mistakes that cursed our finances in the past. We will not give the enemy an open door by robbing You in tithes and offerings. We will be faithful with the few things we have and I know You will make us ruler over many more things. I stand on Your promise that when we give, it will be given unto us pressed down, shaken together and running over. Lord, condition us to give cheerfully and know that the harvest is always greater than the seed sown. Father, You charged those who are rich in this world to not be high-minded or trust in uncertain riches, but to trust in You, the living God who gives us richly all things to enjoy. I declare we are ready to distribute and willing to share the good things You give us. We will not be like the man who was disappointed when Jesus said to follow him, sell his possessions, and give to the poor so that he would have treasure in heaven. I declare nothing we have is so important that we would not let it go in service to You. Father, I ask You for wisdom to help us be good stewards with money and possessions. Guide us in our spending and help us sow into good ground, in the right season. You alone are able to make all grace abound toward us so we will have sufficiency in all things and abound in every good work. Father, help us prepare for increase and purpose it to advance Your kingdom. Thank You for blessing us abundantly. Thank You for the overflow to bless others. From this day forward, my husband and I will seek first Your kingdom and Your righteousness and everything we need will be added unto us. Thank You for setting our thinking and our finances in order today. I am in agreement with these women of God and I believe what we've asked for is done in the name of Jesus, Amen.

Confessions

My husband and I are not high-minded. We do not trust in uncertain riches. We trust in the living God who gives us richly all things to enjoy. We are rich in good works, ready to distribute, and willing to share what God gives us. We prepare a good foundation for ourselves against the time to come so we may lay hold on eternal life. (1 Tim 6:17-19)

My husband and I bring our tithes into the storehouse. God opens the windows of heaven and pours out a blessing for us that there is not room enough to receive. (Malachi 3:10)

God, who provides seed and bread for us, will also provide and multiply our resources for sowing and increase the fruits of our righteousness. We will be enriched in all things and in every way so that we can be generous. As we administer generosity, it will bring forth thanksgiving to God. (2 Corinthians 9:10-11)

Day 5 Intimacy

Father God, I come to You, in the name of Jesus, to pray for an increase of intimacy in my marriage. I ask You to reveal any barriers that currently exist between us so I can break them down and never allow them to arise again. Lord, deliver us from their effects, known and unknown. Right now I destroy all ungodly soul ties from past intimate experiences and relationships. I declare those old memories and habits may no longer harm our marriage. I pray for an inner healing. I cast down our old thoughts about what intimacy is and I ask You to teach us the truth. Help us define romance, intimacy, and sex as You do and not as the world does. Train us to love fervently with a pure heart as You knit our hearts together in love. Help me satisfy my husband at all times and delight him with my love. Work through me to demonstrate Your love for him. Teach me ways to show him how special he is. I know that what I think of him and what I say to him impacts how he sees himself. Father, help me ensure my thoughts, words, and actions convey how much I support him and believe that he will succeed. Help him trust me and know he can safely confide in me. Condition me to never misuse this position of trust. Help me know what blesses him and remember to do those things often. Lord, I ask You to inspire my husband romantically. Show him how to touch my heart through his words and actions. Help me reveal my desires in a way that is not demanding but also doesn't make them a huge mystery that he is expected to solve. Quicken me to notice and appreciate the little things he does for me. Lord, help us make our intimacy fulfilling, enjoyable, freeing, and refreshing. Quicken me to prepare myself physically, mentally, and emotionally to meet my husband's needs. Train us to not deprive each other of intimacy. Father, I repent for any time I've denied him in the past and I ask You to forgive me. Heal my heart where it has been hardened towards my husband.

Right now I forgive him for every hurtful thing he's ever said or done to me. I release us from every offense and I call forth reconciliation and healing between us. Lord, condition us to demonstrate our affection in a manner that glorifies You. I declare, from this day forward, we will treasure and guard our intimacy as a special connection between us that no one else can partake in. I proclaim we are delivered from things that would encourage us to neglect this vital area of our marriage. We will remain far from things and people that would tempt us to be untrue. Lord, train us to remain sexually pure and not sin against our bodies with immoral thoughts, words or deeds. I know marriage is honorable in all and the bed is undefiled. Today I say no impurity will taint what You joined together. I proclaim my marriage is free from the desire to look outward for stimulation and fulfillment. I declare our sexual desire is only for each other and we will not be deceived by the enemy's tricks to lure us away. We will hearken unto Your voice showing us the way out of temptation. Above all, I ask You to condition us to worship You as our first love. I know it is only then that we are able to love each other effectively. I commit this area of our marriage to You. I am in agreement with these women of God and I believe what we've asked for is done in the name of Jesus, Amen.

Confessions

My body belongs to my husband and his body belongs to me. We will not deny each other except for mutual consent while fasting. Then we will resume marital relations so satan cannot tempt us due to a lack of self-control. (1 Corinthians 7: 4-5) My husband and I desire each other. (Song of Solomon 7:10) Like an apple tree among the trees of the woods, so is my husband among other men. I delight to sit in his shadow. His fruit is sweet to me. He brings me to the banquet house and waves a banner of love over me. I am comforted when I am near him. (Song of Solomon 2:3-4)

Day 6 Order

Father God, I come to You, in the name of Jesus, to pray for Your order in my marriage. Lord, I ask You to start with me because I know when I am not in order I hinder my husband, my home, and our family from being in order. I believe You placed my husband as the head of our home. Help me to not hinder him from occupying and operating in this place of leadership. I know a wise woman builds her house but a foolish woman tears her house down with her own hands. Lord, show me where I have caused destruction in my home. I repent for everything I've ever said or done that hurt my husband. I know my thoughts and words about him affect his thoughts about himself. Lord, help me to never take this lightly. Condition me to honor my husband as the head. Remind me that when I honor Your son, I am honoring You. Quicken me to always build him up and never tear him down. Lord, I repent for the times I was rebellious and not submissive to my husband. Whether it was an obvious, outward act or an internal, hidden resistance, I repent for exalting myself above him as the spiritual leader of our home. Forgive me for disobeying Your word and help me to humble myself. Right now I bind the spirit of error and cut off its ability to twist our thinking. I take into captivity and cast down every worldly idea regarding submission. I declare these ideas can no longer distort our thinking. Lord, I ask for understanding of the importance of submitting to my husband in obedience to You. I welcome the spirit of truth to minister to us and align us with Your will. Lord, I believe Your order in our marriage enables You to work freely. Train us to remain in order and unified in Your will. Surround us with holy influences that set a godly example and share wisdom. Father, I ask You to send my husband godly counsel to help him lead our family. Condition him to submit to You and trust

You to guide him as the head of our home. I decree he has confidence leading our family because he knows that You chose him for this position and You will not abandon him. I call forth the spirit of wisdom and the spirit of peace to help him make decisions. I know the steps of a good man are ordered by You. I declare my husband walks boldly in the steps You've ordered for him. Thank You for answering him when he seeks You. Father, condition us to be sensitive to Your voice, trust You, and obey Your instruction. Thank You for restoring Your order in my marriage. I am in agreement with these women of God and I believe what we've asked for is done in the name of Jesus, Amen.

Confessions

I submit to my husband in reverence to the Lord. He is the head of me even as Christ is head of the church and Savior of the body. I am subject to my husband in everything. He loves me as Christ loves the church and gave Himself for it. (Ephesians 5:22-25)

Through wisdom my life, my family, and my home are built. By understanding they are established and set on a good foundation. By knowledge every area is filled with all precious and pleasant riches. (Proverbs 24: 3-4)

I live in harmony with my husband. I am not haughty. I adjust and give myself to humble tasks. (Romans 12:16)

Our speech is always with grace and seasoned with salt so we may know how to answer every man. (Colossians 4:6)

Day 7 The Home

Father God, I come to You, in the name of Jesus, to pray Your will be done in our home. I dedicate and consecrate my home as a sanctuary for You to dwell in and work through. Lord, help us make it a safe haven that builds up our family by Your Spirit. Train us to be good stewards over the house You've given us. Help us build our home with Your word as the foundation. I present our home to You for examination today. I ask for Your light to come and reveal all darkness. Uncover any idol, reminder of past sin, movie, or music that glorifies sin and anything else that has opened the door to darkness. No matter what we paid or how much importance I once placed on these things, I commit to rid our home of them today. Whatever has hindered Your presence from dwelling in any inch of my home, I bind it and cast it out in the name of Jesus. Help me to never do anything that would disturb the sanctuary-like qualities You establish here. Father, help me maintain this home. I ask for grace, strength, energy, and motivation to keep my home clean, anointed, and protected. Lord, help me remember that I am a steward over my house and everything I do to maintain it is unto You. I know that You are not unjust to forget my work and labor of love in Your name. Thank You for giving Your angels charge over us to keep us in all our ways. I ask You to assign Your angels to guard every entrance to my home and block access to anything that desires to disrupt the peace and harmony. I decree no sickness, terror, or plague will come near my home. Every night my family and our guests will have safety and peaceful sleep. Lord, quicken me to welcome You all day long with praise, worship, and prayer. I desire that my family and our guests sense Your presence as they enter our home and it compels them to surrender more to You. Father, use my home as a vessel that feeds them in their body and spirit. I

24

pray You make a way for me to be home to greet my husband when he arrives each day. Help me express how much I appreciate and miss him. Help him look forward to coming home. I rebuke the desire for us to look outside for acceptance, enjoyment, and comfort. From this point forward, we will always find those things here in our home with You. I commit to maintain a nurturing atmosphere in our home that ministers love, restoration, mercy, and grace. All who enter in will know that You are the Lord of our home. Father, I ask You to place Your name on our home today. I am in agreement with these women of God and I believe what we've asked for is done in the name of Jesus, Amen.

Confessions

As for me and my house, we will serve the Lord. (Joshua 24:15)

God is not unjust to forget my work and labor of love. In this I minister to the saints. (Hebrews 6:10)

Through wisdom our home is built. By understanding it is established. By knowledge the chambers are filled with all precious and pleasant riches. (Proverbs 24: 3-4)

Day 8 The Mind

Father God, I come to You, in the name of Jesus, to pray for growth and renewing in my mind and in my husband's mind. Condition us to clearly discern between Your voice and any other. Bring to light all of the beliefs we've been taught in the past that are contrary to Your word. No matter who taught us or how much confidence we once held in those erroneous beliefs, I cast them down today. You taught me that if I have faith as a grain of mustard seed I can tell a mountain to move and it has to move. Some of these beliefs seem like mountains to me because they've been there for so long. I declare today is a turning point. In the name of Jesus, I command those erroneous and destructive beliefs to be removed and cast into the sea. Father, train us to use our spiritual weapons skillfully to capture every thought and bring it to the obedience of Christ while casting down every imagination and high thing that exalts itself against the knowledge of You. I declare, from this day forward, Your word is the ultimate authority in our minds. The voice of our flesh and the voice of the enemy are drowned out and disproved. I call forth a hunger for Your word that compels us to study to show ourselves approved to You. Train us to put on Your whole armor and become skillful with the sword of the Spirit. I know we don't fight against flesh and blood but against powers, principalities, rulers of the darkness, and spiritual wickedness in high places. We do not war according to the flesh because our warfare is not carnal but mighty through You to pull down strongholds. I declare my husband and I are now turning our warfare away from one another. We are joining forces as one, strong in You and in the power of Your might, against the evil one. With Your armor, we are able to stand against the wiles of the devil. Lord, You gave us power and authority over all the enemy's power and You promised that nothing shall by any means harm us. With this knowledge and authority, I bind all lying spirits and command them away from us. I welcome the spirit of truth to rule and reign in us. Lord, thank You for giving us the spirit of power, of love, and of a sound mind. I decree we will no longer allow impure, corrupt, or sinful thoughts to torment us. I rebuke every fiery dart from the adversary and I lift up the shield of faith to cover and protect us from now on. I declare my husband and I operate with the mind of Christ in power, love, and soundness. Lord, thank You for continually renewing our minds with Your word. Train us to communicate clearly and remove the enemy's chance to enter in with confusion. I know that just as he attempts to twist Your words he will also attempt to twist ours. Thank You for revealing satan's devices so we are not ignorant of them. Father, quicken us to pray for each other in every situation. I decree from now on we will trust You and keep our minds on You. Thank You for Your promise to keep us in perfect peace that surpasses understanding. We program our minds to think on things that are true, noble, just, pure, lovely, of a good report, and virtuous. I declare our thoughts and beliefs now fully agree with Your word. The old has passed away and all things have become new. I am in agreement with these women of God and I believe we've received what we've asked for in the name of Jesus, Amen.

Confessions

My husband and I are not conformed to this world. We are transformed by the renewing of our minds so we may prove the perfect will of God. (Romans 12:2)
My husband and I are spiritually minded. We receive life and peace. (Romans 8:6)
The peace of God, which surpasses all understanding, keeps our hearts and minds through Christ Jesus. (Philippians 4:7)
God keeps us in perfect peace because we keep our minds on Him and trust Him. (Isaiah 26:3)

Day 9 Jealousy and Coveting

Father God, I come to You, in the name of Jesus, to pray for deliverance from all jealousy and covetousness. The world encourages us to want more and more possessions. We are constantly provoked to be unsatisfied with what we have and to want what others have. I call out that belief as a lie because it is contrary to Your word. You commanded us to not covet our neighbor's house, spouse, possessions, or anything that belongs to them. You taught that covetousness is idolatry. Lord, I repent for every jealous and covetous thought I've ever had. Forgive me for worshipping or adoring anything aside from You. Forgive me for not opening my eyes to all that You have done in my life. Forgive me for belittling what You've given me by comparing it to others' possessions. I receive Your forgiveness and I call forth a change in my mindset. I am so thankful for every work You've done in and for us. Father, Your works are priceless, incomparable, and not measured according to what You've done for someone else. Your work was designed uniquely for restoration and increase in my family and marriage. What You provide is not only sufficient for us but it is above and beyond what we could ever ask or think because it is the perfect supply. I decree we will no longer desire things outside of Your will, no matter how appealing they appear. From this point forward, I set my spirit as the leader and director of my flesh. I declare we are no longer drawn to the things of this world that birthed envy and jealousy in the past. You taught that those who measure and compare themselves among themselves are without understanding and are not wise. I know that jealousy and envy make people bitter and cause confusion, disharmony, and all sorts of evil work. This is opposite of what I desire. I come to You continuously seeking understanding and wisdom. Right now I bind the spirit of jealousy and command it away from us forever. Jealousy, covetousness, and envy will no longer hinder us from receiving understanding, wisdom, harmony, clarity, contentment, and peace. I proclaim we now have thankful hearts that worship You for all You are and all You've done. What more can we ask for above having Your hand upon us? We can do all things through Christ which strengthens us. We are amply supplied because You supply everything we need according to Your riches and glory. I decree we are content because our confidence is in You as our source. Thank You for leading us. We receive Your wisdom, direction, light, and understanding in every situation. I am in agreement with these women of God and I believe what we've asked for is done in the name of Jesus, Amen.

Confessions

My husband and I are blessed in the city and in the fields. We are blessed coming in and going out. All the work of our hands is blessed. We are the head and not the tail; above and never beneath. (Deuteronomy 28:2-14)

My husband and I delight in God's commandments. Our hearts are inclined to His testimonies and not to covetousness. We turn away our eyes from beholding vanity and God quickens us in His way. (Psalm 119:35-37)

My husband and I have God's love in us. This love endures long and is patient and kind. This love is not envious or boiling over with jealousy. This love is not boastful or conceited. This love is not arrogant, selfish, or easily provoked. This love does not rejoice at injustice or unrighteousness but only rejoices in the truth. With God's love, we bear all things, believe the best of every person, and hope in all circumstances. This love endures all things without weakening and does not fail. (1 Corinthians 13:4-8)

Day 10 Trust

Father God, I come to You, in the name of Jesus, to pray for an increase of trust in my marriage. I recognize the only way to do this is for both of us to trust You more. In-turn, You will mold us into trustworthy vessels. Lord, I repent for the times I have not been trustworthy. I declare I will be forthright and honest from this day forward. If I've denied trust to my husband because of something someone else has done, I repent. I forgive the person that hurt me and I am set free from the bondage of that hurt today. I will not continue to project onto my husband and punish him for others' mistakes. Father, help him to do the same for me. In the areas where we have broken trust with each other, help us to reestablish it. Right now I release and forgive my husband for every untrustworthy thing he's ever said or done. Help him to forgive me for the things I've said and done also. Lord, condition us to walk in integrity and trust in You. Thank You for giving us the spirit of truth to guide us into all truth and show us things to come. I will keep my mind and eyes on You and I know You will guide us with Your eye and keep us in perfect peace. Today I bind mercy and truth around our necks and write them on the tablet of our hearts so we will find favor in Your sight and with one another. You taught us to put our trust in You and not in man. Lord, quicken us to not focus on trusting each other, but rather trusting Your Spirit within us. From this day forward, we will trust You instead of relying on our own understanding. We will acknowledge You in all things and boldly walk in the path You direct for us. Your word is a lamp for our feet and a light for our path. I decree we will follow where You lead. Thank You for cleansing me from all wrong thinking about trust today and creating in me a clean heart and a new revelation that yields good fruit. Lord, I trust You and I thank You for being trustworthy. I am in agreement with these women of God and I believe what we've asked for is done in the name of Jesus, Amen.

Confessions

My husband and I have a good and clear conscience. We walk uprightly and live nobly in complete honesty in all things. (Hebrews 13: 18)

The heart of my husband safely trusts me. I will do him good and not evil all the days of my life. (Proverbs 31:11-12)

My husband and I are blessed because we make the Lord our refuge and our trust. (Psalm 40: 4)

My husband and I trust in the Lord with all our heart and we lean not into our own understanding. We acknowledge Him in all our ways and He directs our path. (Proverbs 3:5)

Day 11 Fear

Father God, I come to You, in the name of Jesus, to pray for all fear to be removed from my marriage. You taught that there is no fear in love; but perfect love casts out fear. Fear brings torment and whoever is afraid has not reached the full maturity of love. Lord, train us to perfect our love for You and love for each other so that all fear may be cast out. Mature our understanding of love and how to operate in it. I decree we are free from the fear of man and all the torment that came with it. Lord, condition us to rise above the criticism and opinions of others. Our only concern is to please You. Condition me to speak Your word over myself and my husband to build us up every day. I say we are strong in You, established in righteousness, far from oppression, and we do not fear terror because You said it shall not come near our dwelling. I decree in all things we are more than conquerors through Christ Jesus. I am sure, without a doubt, that neither death nor life, nor angels, nor principalities, nor powers, nor things present, nor things to come, nor height, nor depth, nor any other creature shall be able to separate us from Your love. As long as my husband and I stay close to You and keep our eyes on You, fear cannot enter into our marriage and separate us. Lord, quicken me to rise up every day and confess that You are my light, my salvation, and the strength of my life so I shall not be afraid. Train us to quickly recognize the ploy of the enemy. Father, help us remember Your word and speak it over those ploys and declare them fruitless. In the name of Jesus, I bind the spirit of fear and declare it has no place in us. I welcome the spirit of power, of love, and of a sound mind in our lives. Lord, I choose to only receive what You give us. We do not receive the fear of man, fear of failure, fear of the enemy, or fear of temptation because we recognize these things come from the enemy and are meant to steal, kill, and destroy. I declare fear will now be an uncomfortable presence for us. It will be treated as an unwelcome trespasser. We will speak to it with the authority in Your word and command it to vacate our presence immediately. We will not be anxious about anything, but instead we will bring all our concerns to You in prayer and trust You to direct our path. Thank You for giving us Your peace that surpasses all understanding. I receive it now. Thank You for keeping us in Your shadow, protected from harm. You are the greatest protection that exists and I am just thankful to be Your daughter. I am in agreement with these women of God and I believe what we've asked for is done in the name of Jesus, Amen.

Confessions

My husband and I fear no evil because God is with us. His rod of protection and staff of guidance comfort us. (Psalm 23:4)
My husband and I are not afraid of sudden terror or panic because the Lord is our confidence. God keeps us from being caught in a trap or any hidden danger. (Proverbs 3:25-26)
Our trust is in God. We are not afraid of what man can do to us. (Psalm 56:11)
My husband and I have peace. Not the peace of this world, but the peace of the Father. Our hearts are not troubled and we are not afraid. (John 14:27)

Day 12 Protection

Father God, I come to You, in the name of Jesus, to pray for Your hand of protection over my marriage. I know that when we obey and trust You, no evil, sickness, or disease shall come near us. You have given Your angels special charge over us to accompany, defend, and preserve us. Lord, train us to dwell with You in the protection of Your shadow so You can shield us from all danger. Condition us to stay near to You at all times. Right now I cancel all the plans that sought to destroy our lives, our marriage, and our health. Lord, train us to care for our bodies as the temple of the Holy Spirit. I call forth an increase in motivation and discipline to exercise and maintain a healthy diet. Father, quicken us to enter into Your rest each evening so we are rejuvenated every morning. I repent for every time I refused Your rest and I ask You to forgive me. We will no longer take the health You've given us for granted. I declare we will preserve our health by being good stewards over our bodies. In return, we receive Your promise to restore our health, heal our wounds, and provide peaceful sleep. My husband and I put on the whole armor of God so we will be able to stand against the adversary. We put on the belt of truth and the breastplate of integrity and righteousness. We shod our feet with the gospel of peace. We lift up the shield of faith that quenches all the fiery darts of the wicked. We put on the helmet of salvation and we take up the sword of the spirit which is Your word. We will pray at all times in the spirit so we may stay alert, persevere and intercede effectively. With all of Your armor, I declare no evil shall overcome us or enter our dwelling and no weapon formed against us shall prosper. Father, thank You for giving us power to tread upon serpents, scorpions, and over all the power of the enemy. Thank You for declaring that nothing shall by any means harm us. Above all, thank You for writing our names in heaven. I completely trust You above anything and anyone. I declare my husband and I will listen to, know, and follow Your voice and not the voice of a stranger. We will study and renew our minds daily with Your word for without it we are defenseless. I pray for revelation, understanding, and discernment as we study Your word and learn who You are, who we are in You, and what You've promised us. Thank You for establishing us in righteousness and protecting us. I cast down all fearful thoughts that come against this knowledge. I call forth the spirit of truth to teach us all the things You spoke about us. Thank You for giving us instruction and weaponry to stand strong and overcome without fear. Thank You for hearing my petition, empowering us with Your word, and protecting us with Your mighty hand. I truly believe my marriage is protected from all harm from this day forward. I am in agreement with these women of God and I believe what we've asked for is done in the name of Jesus, Amen.

Confessions

My husband and I call upon God and He answers us. He is with us in trouble and He delivers us. He satisfies us with long life and salvation. (Psalm 91: 15-16)

God is our rock, our fortress, and our deliverer. God is our strength and we trust in Him. He is our buckler and our high tower. We call upon the Lord and He saves us from our enemies. (Psalm 18:2-3)

Because my husband and I have made the Lord our refuge and dwelling place, no evil shall befall us and no plague shall enter our dwelling. God's angels have charge over us to keep us in all our ways. They bear us up and prevent us from striking our foot against a stone. (Psalm 91:9-12)

Day 13 Lusts of the Flesh

Father God, I come to You, in the name of Jesus, to pray for deliverance from the lust of our flesh. Lord, I ask You to reveal any lusts of the flesh operating in my marriage. You taught that the desires of our flesh oppose the Holy Spirit and vice versa. That the works of the flesh are immorality, adultery, impurity, indecency, idolatry, witchcraft, hate, jealousy, anger, selfishness, division, heresies, envy, murder, and drunkenness. Even if a person looks upon another with lust to do these things, it is sin and they will not inherit Your kingdom. We desperately desire to inherit Your kingdom therefore I repent for any works of the flesh in my marriage and I receive Your forgiveness. Right now my husband and I clothe ourselves with the Lord Jesus Christ and we no longer make provision to fulfill the lust of our flesh. Lord, open our eyes to understand the new creation You've made us. Help us to quit taking back that old un-renewed self that tries to corrupt through lusts and delusions. I know lust keeps us from understanding Your word because it shuts our ears to You and opens them to the adversary. Right now I tear down every stronghold of lust and I bind all perverse spirits. I call forth deliverance from immoral and sexual lust. We no longer love or cherish the world or the things in it like the lust of the flesh, the lust of the eyes, and the pride of life because those things do not come from You. I declare we no longer lust after beauty and we are not captured by eyes that seduce. We will not be lured by evil plans or flattering words of loose people. In the name of Jesus, I bind the seducing spirit manifesting itself in words, publications, movies, and pictures. I command it to go and never return. I proclaim, from this day forward, we will not seek out those things that lead us into temptation. If a questionable situation arises, we will immediately seek and follow You. You do not lead us into temptation, but You deliver us from evil. You always provide a way out of temptation. Condition us to be more sensitive to Your voice so we will always recognize Your warnings. Father, forgive me if I have ever selfishly caused any man to lust for me. I understand my body is naturally beautiful and attractive. I will not use this knowledge to entice, control, or attract men in a lustful way. My body was not made to be used as an instrument of wickedness. It was bought by the blood of Jesus to be the temple of the Holy Spirit. I commit to adorn myself with clothes that glorify You and aren't seductive or luring. When people notice me, I desire it be because they are drawn to the Holy Spirit within me. Lord, train us to walk in the Spirit so we will not fulfill the lusts of our flesh. Condition us to crucify our flesh daily so we will not sow into it and reap corruption. Right now I receive the spirit of liberty and I declare we are free from desiring things that falsely satisfied us in the past. I call forth a hunger for righteousness and a desire for the fruit of the Spirit to manifest in our lives. Train us to sow to the Spirit and reap everlasting life of the Spirit. Quicken us to diligently guard our hearts and minds through prayer and cast down everything that is contrary to Your word. Lord, thank You for revelation knowledge that renews our minds and sets us on the path You predestined for us. I am in agreement with these women of God and I believe what we've asked for is done in the name of Jesus, Amen.

Confessions

My husband and I are free from our old, un-renewed selves that once characterized us. We are no longer corrupted by lusts and desires that spring from delusion. We are renewed in our minds and have a fresh attitude. (Ephesians 4:21-23)
We are dead to sin and alive in unbroken fellowship with God. Sin does not rule in our bodies. We do not allow our bodies to be vessels for wickedness. We offer and yield them as instruments of righteousness to God. (Romans 6:11-13)

Day 14 Priorities

Father God, I come to You, in the name of Jesus, to ask for help to get our priorities in order. I know every person must choose who they will serve. Lord, I boldly declare that as for me and my house, we will serve You. Help me to ensure my actions line up with my confession. I declare our relationship with You is the number one priority in life. Without You, we can do nothing. Father, condition us to set aside ample and quality time to read Your word, pray, and worship You every single day. Show us how to worship and pray without ceasing. I know as we do this, You will maximize our time and ability to accomplish everything that needs to be done. You taught that no one can serve two masters; for either he will hate the one and love the other, or else he will be loyal to one and despise the other. Lord, You are our Master. I repent for every time I put other things before or above You. Thank You for forgiving me. I love You and I desire to be loyal to You in everything I say and do. Nothing is more important to me than being in Your will. Lord, I surrender to You and I ask You to have Your way in my life, in my husband's life and in our marriage. You are my first love and I whole-heartedly return to You. I know that the earth and everything in it belongs to You. I once considered time, husband, house, children, money, and body to be mine. Now I understand that those things were never mine because they were always Yours and will always be Yours. Father, condition us to be good stewards over what You've placed in our care. Help us treat everyone and everything in a manner that glorifies You. Train us to redeem the time and not waste it on things that are not of You and have no eternal purpose. I ask for grace to balance being a spouse and parent, running a home, working, and serving. Quicken us to frequently check with You to ensure we are only taking on what You called us to do. I know with

You all things are possible and You will not put more on us than we can bear. Condition us to rely on Your grace to accomplish all we have to do each day. Lord, I surrender and ask You to mold me into the wife, woman, mother, homemaker, sister, daughter, friend, and neighbor You predestined me to be. There is no way I can successfully do this in my own strength or ability. I need Your grace. When I feel overwhelmed with the "To Do" list, remind me to return to and rely on Your grace. I don't even need to understand how so much was done, so gracefully, in so little time. I will just lift my hands and my voice to praise You because You are my help. Help me to properly place my husband right after You to ensure that he is never neglected. I ask You to be the Lord of my marriage. Guide us in preserving our covenant with You and our covenant with each other. Thank You for hearing me today. Thank You for lifting this burden of trying to prioritize and control everything myself. Thank You for instruction and encouragement. Thank You for opening the eyes of our understanding today. I am in agreement with these women of God and I believe we've received what we've asked for in the name of Jesus, Amen.

Confessions

My husband and I seek first God's kingdom and His righteousness and everything we need is added to us. (Matthew 6:33)
The Lord builds our house. Our labor is not in vain. (Psalm 127:1)
Jesus has priority over us. He existed before us. He advanced before us because He is our chief. From the fullness of His grace, we receive blessings upon blessings, favor upon favor, and gifts upon gifts. (1 John 1:15-16)

Day 15 Communication

Father God, I come to You, in the name of Jesus, to pray for excellent communication in my marriage. I know that words can either build up or tear down because death and life are in the power of the tongue. Lord, condition us to only speak words that build up and bring life to our marriage. I confess and repent for the times I spoke to my husband in a critical, nagging, and accusing manner. Forgive me for selfishly speaking to him in a degrading tone just to prove I am right. I repent for not honoring him. I receive Your forgiveness and ask You to train us to communicate in a manner that pleases You. Quicken us to speak from the sound mind You gave us and communicate without the cloud of negative emotions. Father, help me understand my husband's heart as he communicates with me. I forgive him for every hurtful thing he's ever said to me. I will no longer replay those words over and over in my mind. No good thing comes from thinking about those words and holding my husband hostage emotionally for what he has said to me in the past. I forgive him from my heart today. I declare the enemy may no longer use those memories to corrupt my thinking and harden my heart towards my husband. Lord, You taught that the heart of the righteous studies how to answer, but the mouth of the wicked pours forth evil. From this day forward, I will consider my words before I speak. If I do not know how to reply kindly, I will seek You for the answer. You taught that a soft answer turns away wrath but harsh words stir up anger. Condition us to align our words with Your word so that no corrupt words proceed out of our mouths, but only those that are soft, kind, good, and build up. Lord, convict us quickly if we begin to complain, use negative language, or speak words that are contrary to Your word. Help us remember and speak Your word so we bring forth life instead of death. Train us to communicate in respect and love. Set guards before our mouths and keep the door of our lips. Right now I cancel our old communication habits and replace them with those that contain Your wisdom, grace, and life. Today is a new day. I will bless my husband with every word that leaves my mouth concerning him. Father, I trust that You have begun a new work in me, my husband and my marriage. I believe You will continue developing and perfecting that work until it is completed. Thank You for transforming me so I no longer hinder Your work in my husband and my marriage. I am in agreement with these women of God and I believe what we've asked for is done in the name of Jesus, Amen.

Confessions

My husband and I let no corrupt communication proceed out of our mouths. We only speak that which is good to edify and minister grace to the hearers. (Ephesians 4:29)

My husband and I desire to live good and long lives. We keep our tongues from evil and our lips from speaking deceit. (Psalm 34:12-13)

My husband and I have life in the power of our tongues. We bring life with our words and we will eat the fruit thereof. (Proverbs 18:21)

I keep my mouth and tongue and therefore I keep my soul from trouble. (Proverbs 21:23)

Day 16 Relationships

Father God, I come to You, in the name of Jesus, to pray for strong, healthy relationships with others. Help my husband and I recognize the people You've already placed in our lives. Condition us to value the relationships with our brethren in Christ as special and set apart from others. I ask You to send wise men of integrity to counsel my husband in truth and not flattery. I declare we will no longer be influenced by people that do not add to our lives in any good way. When those people cross our paths, we will be godly influences that lead them to You. Lord, I ask You to send me mature sisters to strengthen and encourage me and teach me how to love my family and care for myself and my home. Right now I bind all competitiveness and insecurity and I cast it down forever. I call forth trust so we can openly share our hearts and learn from one another. Father, mold me into the true friend You predestined me to be. Reveal any relationships that are not bearing good fruit in our lives. Surround us with believing, married couples to fellowship with and learn from. I pray Your will be done in our marriage so Your glory may be seen through us and be a testimony of Your goodness. I pray for healthy and peaceful relationships with all of our family members. In the name of Jesus, I bind all spirits that have caused division in my family. I call forth reconciliation and brotherly love. Lord, I ask You to restore relationships that we once thought were hopeless. You taught that he who hates his brother is in darkness and does not know where he is going because the darkness has blinded his eyes. Today I decree we will forgive others as You have forgiven us and we will no longer be blinded. Father, I confess all unforgiveness in my heart. I repent and I receive Your forgiveness. Help us always remember how You've forgiven us and let that be our example of how to forgive others. Right now I call forth the spirit of liberty to set us free from the bondage and damage associated with unforgiveness. Lord, help us remember that forgiveness doesn't make the other person right; it makes us free so our prayers will not be hindered. As we have forgiven them, I declare we will no longer show contempt for them or try to repay them for what they did. Lord, I pray that their eyes are opened and they seek You for forgiveness. I decree, from this day forward, my husband and I will bless those who curse us, do good to those who hate us, and pray for those who spitefully use and persecute us. I declare my husband and I will honor our father and mother so that we will have long, good lives. Lord, train us to be a light that draws others to You. Thank You for giving us grace to love others the way You love us and forgive others the way You forgive us. Help us to rely on Your grace and not our own ability. I am in agreement with these women of God and I believe what we've asked for is done in the mighty name of Jesus, Amen.

Confessions

My husband and I provoke one another unto love and good works. We do not forsake the assembling of ourselves together but we exhort one another more and more as we draw closer to the day Jesus will return. (Hebrews 10:24-25)

My husband and I love others as God loves us. By this they know we are disciples of God. (John 13:34-35)

All bitterness, wrath, anger, and evil-speaking are put away from us. We are kind to one another and tenderhearted. We forgive one another as God, for Christ's sake, forgave us. (Ephesians 4:31-32)

We walk in the light as He is in the light and we have fellowship one with another. (1 John 1:7)

Day 17 Attitude

Father God, I come to You, in the name of Jesus, to pray for an attitude adjustment. I believe You are preparing us for the plans You have for our future. Help us receive Your plans and walk in them with merry hearts and an attitude that glorifies You. No matter what I was taught in the past, I understand now that I am able to control my attitude. Lord, I confess and repent for every time I allowed people or circumstances to influence my attitude and I said or did things that were not pleasing to You. Forgive me for allowing my flesh to lead me and forfeit the joy and peace You gave me. I receive Your forgiveness today and I take authority over my attitude from this day forward. In the name of Jesus, I pull down the strongholds that provoke us to have a negative attitude. I declare they will no longer influence our attitude and send us on an emotional roller coaster. I welcome the spirit of power, of love, and of a sound mind to direct our attitude each day. Lord, condition us to stay in the Spirit and respond in love at all times. I know we have joy by the answer of our mouth. Train us to speak words that bring life and minister joy. You taught that a good man out of the good treasure of his heart brings forth good; and an evil man out of the evil treasure of his heart brings forth evil because his mouth speaks out of the abundance of his heart. Lord, help us to get our hearts right with You and filled with Your word so every word we speak brings forth life, goodness, and joy. Help us maintain merry hearts that provoke us to have a good attitude at all times. You taught that a merry heart makes a cheerful countenance. I pray our cheerful countenance shines Your light in the atmosphere everywhere we go. I decree in every conversation we will speak words that minister grace to the hearers around us. I declare we will not allow situations or other people to set the tone. We will make room for Your Spirit to establish an atmosphere that glorifies You and establishes Your will on the earth. I declare my husband and I lay aside every weight and we patiently run the race that You've set before us. I ask You to give us a vision of Your plan for us so we may focus on it and not be distracted or weighed down by the cares of the world. Help us understand Your purpose for having us where we are right now. Thank You for empowering us to bloom right where You planted us. I decree we are steadfast knowing that You have begun a good work in us and You will continue until it is completed. We will keep our eyes on You and receive Your peace and inner tranquility that prevails no matter what goes on around us. I decree that today is the day to rejoice and be glad. Not "whenever this or that happens" but today. Lord, I rejoice in You today. I receive Your promises today. Thank You for placing us above and never beneath. Thank You for giving us a new perspective and a new attitude that glorifies You. I am in agreement with these women of God and I believe what we've asked for is done in the matchless name of Jesus, Amen.

Confessions

My husband and I are not conformed to this world. We are transformed by the renewing of our minds so we may prove the good, acceptable, and perfect will of God. (Romans 12:2)
Out of the good treasure of our hearts, my husband and I bring forth that which is good. (Luke 6:45)
I have a merry heart and a cheerful countenance. I do not have sorrow in my heart. My spirit is whole. (Proverbs 15:13)

Day 18 Deliverance

Father God, I come to You, in the name of Jesus, to pray for manifestation of deliverance in every area of my marriage. You promised that when we call upon You in the day of trouble, You will deliver us. Lord, I set my love upon You and thank You for Your promise to deliver us and set us on high because we know You. Thank You for the complete work You did on Calvary to deliver us once and for all. I know that whom the Son set free is free indeed. I ask You to reveal any area of my life where I am not walking in the freedom and deliverance You paid such a high price for. I confess and repent for every time I've allowed myself to get entangled again in the yoke of bondage. I call forth Your anointing, right now, to destroy every yoke of bondage that has been placed upon us. In the name of Jesus, I bind the spirit of bondage and I call forth the spirit of liberty to manifest the freedom You gave us. Thank You for giving us mighty weapons in the spiritual realm to pull down strongholds and cast down imaginations and everything that exalts itself against Your word. Right now, I take all our thoughts captive and bring them to the obedience of Your word. I declare my husband and I will not live in or suffer from bondage another day. In the name of Jesus, I cast out all hurtful memories of the past, generational curses, plans of the enemy, unforgiveness, and anything else that once held us captive. I decree we are not ignorant of satan's devices. Father, I ask You to reveal any weak area in our lives so we may build it up through Your word and prevent the enemy from entering in. I command a cease to every routine and destructive habit that once caused division. I declare, from this day forward, my husband and I will stand fast in the liberty by which Christ made us free and we will never be entangled again with the yoke of bondage. Lord, I ask You to restore everything that has been stolen from us. Condition us to remain free by putting on Your armor and using it skillfully to protect us and accomplish Your will. I decree my husband and I forget those things which are behind and we reach toward the goal of the prize of Your high calling in Christ Jesus. Father, train us to boldly and faithfully proclaim what You have already done and call those things that are not yet seen, as though they were. I ask for the spirit of wisdom to minister to us daily, reveal all things, and deliver us from every evil attack, device, and trap. I decree my husband and I have put on the new nature created in Your image in true righteousness and holiness. We walk in liberty and unity with You. Thank You for setting us free and empowering us to live in freedom. I'm in agreement with these women of God and I believe what we've asked for is done in the name of Jesus, Amen.

Confessions

My husband and I stand fast in the liberty wherewith Christ has made us free. We will not be entangled again with the yoke of bondage. (Galatians 5:1)
The Lord delivers us from every evil work and preserves us for His heavenly kingdom. We glorify God. (2 Timothy 4:18)
The Lord is our rock, our fortress, and our deliverer. He is our strength, our shield, our salvation, our strong hold, and our high tower. We call upon the Lord and we are saved from the enemy. (Psalm 18:2-3)

Day 19 Foundation

Father God, I come to You, in the name of Jesus, to pray for the foundation of my marriage to be strengthened. I know that when we were saved we became citizens in Your household. We joined with other saints and prophets to build a habitation where You live and the foundation is Jesus. Lord, help me understand how this applies to my marriage. You laid a precious Cornerstone for a sure foundation that will not cause shame or give way in panic. This foundation is a rich store of salvation, wisdom, and knowledge. Lord, I want my marriage to be built on Your foundation. If the foundation my marriage rests on now is anything short of this, I forfeit it and ask You to rebuild. You taught that the person who hears Your word and doesn't obey it is like one who built their house on the sand and when the storm hit, it immediately collapsed. But the person who hears and obeys Your word is like one who built their house on a rock and when the storm came it was not moved or shaken because it was secure on the rock. Lord, train us to be doers of Your word and build our marriage on the rock so it will stand strong and secure when the storms hit. Quicken us to dig deeper into Your word so we may be firmly established. Just as a tree is more secure as its roots dig deeper into the soil, I call forth our roots to be so deep in Your word that nothing can sway us or knock us down. Father, I commit to studying Your word daily and I ask You for understanding and revelation knowledge to help us obey Your word and secure our foundation in Christ. Condition us to follow Christ as our Lord so we will remain rooted and built up in Him, strong in the faith, and overflowing with thankfulness. Thank You for establishing us and guarding us from the evil one. Thank You for giving us an everlasting foundation that will not fail. It is in You that we live, move, and have our being. I declare my husband and I are doers of Your word and we will continue in Your way, with a sure foundation, all the days of our lives. I am in agreement with these women of God and I believe we have received what we've asked for in the name of Jesus, Amen.

Confessions

My husband and I are citizens of the household of God. We are built upon the foundation of the apostles and prophets with Christ Himself as the chief Cornerstone. (Ephesians 2:19-20)

The foundation of my marriage is the rock of God's word. When floods arise and storms hit, my marriage will not shake or move because it is securely built and founded on the rock. (Luke 6:48)

God is faithful. He strengthens us, sets us on a firm foundation and guards us from the evil one. (2 Thessalonians 3:3)

Day 20 Obedience

Father God, I come to You, in the name of Jesus, to ask You to help my husband and I live in total obedience to You. I know when much is given, much is required. As we learn Your word, we can either apply it and receive Your promises or disregard it and live in sin under the curse. I know it is sin when a person knows what is right and doesn't do it. As children of obedience to You, I proclaim my husband and I no longer conform ourselves to the evil desires of our former ignorance when our hearts were blind and our understanding was darkened. We are to be holy because You called us and You are holy. Father, I ask You to reveal any disobedience in my life. I repent for everything I've done that was contrary to Your word and I thank You for Your forgiveness. I will no longer allow sin to hinder my prayers or keep us from Your blessings. I ask You to convict my husband of any disobedience in his life and usher in repentance. Show him the harm it does by keeping him from the fullness of You. I call forth a hunger in us for righteousness, holiness, and a right spirit before You. I decree we are now fully consecrated to You. Help us walk in the new nature which You created in righteousness and true holiness. Enlighten the eyes of our understanding so we may comprehend how obedience relates to hope and blessings. As we obey, we will receive peace knowing that our hands are clean, our lives are protected, and You will not withhold any good thing from us. I rebuke the enemy's attempts to make Your way seem too difficult to follow. It's not difficult when we surrender our will for Yours and obey You without hesitation. I know every scripture was breathed and inspired by You. It is profitable for instruction, conviction of sin, and correction of error. Every scripture is for training in righteousness and living in conformity to Your will in thought, purpose, and action so we may be complete and thoroughly equipped for every good work. Lord, condition us to study daily and hide Your word in our hearts so we won't sin against You. Help us see how obeying Your word always adds to and never takes away any good thing in our lives. I bind the lying spirit that tries to convince us otherwise. Lord, train me to intercede for my husband without getting in the way of him receiving from You. I know it is not my responsibility to change him or force him into obedience through nagging and criticizing. I am to pray for him and bless him to help him hear clearly from You. I will not put myself in Your place by trying to convict him. I trust You and I know You can reach him more effectively than I can. I decree from now on my husband and I hearken to Your voice. I'm so thankful Your voice becomes more recognizable and clearer each time we listen and obey You. I declare I am more confident in Your word and more motivated to obey You than ever before. Thank You for seeking me as much as I seek You. I love You and I will obey Your word. I am in agreement with these women of God and I believe what we've asked for is done in the name of Jesus, Amen.

Confessions

My husband and I do not forget God's law. Our hearts keep His commands and we receive long life and peace. Mercy and truth are bound around our necks and written in our hearts. (Proverbs 3:1-3)

We keep God's word and the love of God is perfected in us. Hereby we know that we are in Him. (1 John 2:5)

We are blessed because we obey God's word. (Luke 11:28)

We live in conformity to God's will. We are thoroughly equipped for every good work. (2 Timothy 3:16-17)

My husband and I are purified and obey the truth through the Spirit. We fervently love with pure hearts. We are born again of incorruptible seed, by the word of God which lives and abides forever. (1 Peter 1:22-23)

Day 21 Self-Image

Father God, I come to You, in the name of Jesus, to ask You to help my husband and I see ourselves as You see us. Only You know our true potential because You see the end from the beginning. I recognize that we will never rise above the image we have of ourselves in our own minds. Your ways and thoughts are higher and better than ours. I surrender our self-image to You today and I ask You to continually renew our thoughts about ourselves until they reflect Your thoughts. We are parts of the body of Christ and when every part is working properly, the body grows to full maturity, building itself up in love. Lord, I ask You to show us the spiritual gifts You placed in us to give us confidence in knowing where we fit in the body. Train us to operate in the gifts for Your glory and edify our marriage, church, and community. I recognize as we operate in those gifts in service to You, we will be fulfilled and satisfied knowing that we have a unique and special purpose in Your kingdom. Father, help us replace our old self-image with the new image formed by You. Help us remember to not think more highly of ourselves than we ought to. I know that if we exalt ourselves we will be humbled, but if we humble ourselves we will be exalted. I humble myself therefore under Your mighty hand that You may exalt us in due time. Help us to fully understand that it is not our achievements, how well we perform, how others treat us, or how popular or successful we are that determines our worth. Our value is intrinsic because we are Your children, created after Your image, and redeemed at the highest price. It is not our perfection that gets us through life successfully but it is Your perfection. Help us to really see who You are so we may better understand who we are in Christ Jesus. Condition us to put on the new nature created in Your image, in true righteousness, and holiness. Thank You for continually renewing us after the image and the likeness of You. Thank You that no matter what we've been through in life and no matter how many disappointments we may have suffered, our value in Your eyes remained the same. Thank You for never giving up on us. Lord, I confess and repent for focusing on what I couldn't do and what I didn't have and allowing destructive thoughts to tear-down and corrupt my self-image. From now on, I will choose to focus on what You can do because I know all things are possible with You. In the name of Jesus, I cancel every seed that was planted in the past that negatively impacted my self-image. I decree I will only say things about myself that bring honor to You as my Father and Creator. I proclaim that my husband and I are fearfully and wonderfully made. We have vision and faith to see ourselves as You see us, to receive the good things You have for us, and to become everything that You created us to be. I declare we walk by faith and not by sight. We call those things that are not as though they were. Thank You for aligning our outlook with Yours and revealing who we are in You today. I'm in agreement with these women of God and I believe what we've asked for is done in the name of Jesus, Amen.

Confessions

My husband and I have a fresh mental and spiritual attitude. We put on the new nature which God created in true righteousness and holiness. (Ephesians 4:23-24)
Because we continue to behold the glory of the Lord, as if looking in a mirror, my husband and I are being transfigured into His image from one degree of glory to another, by the Spirit of the Lord. (2 Corinthians 3:18)
God created us in His image. He blessed us and commanded us to be fruitful, multiply, replenish the earth, and subdue it. (Genesis 1:27-28)

Day 22 Purpose

Father God, I come to You, in the name of Jesus, to ask You to reveal Your calling on our lives. I know You've planted eternity, a sense of a purpose, in our hearts and minds which nothing and no one but You can satisfy. I recognize that no matter what we do in life we will be unsatisfied if we are not walking in Your calling for our lives. No matter what plans we had for our lives, I am certain that it is only Your plan that will fully satisfy us and consistently produce fruit. Right now I surrender my will for Yours. I release the expectations and plans I once had for us. I yield to Your calling. I ask for understanding and step by step instructions on how to fully walk in it. I call forth a new hunger within us to study Your word more and spend more quality time in prayer so we will know You more intimately and have the confidence to share Your word with others. I ask You to reveal Your specific calling on our lives. Make it plain so we can understand and run with it. Father, quicken us to not rely on our own strength or ability to fulfill Your call. Help us surrender and allow You to work through us as You supply all our needs. Lord, as we grow in the knowledge of Your calling, train us to follow You and not try to lead. I ask You to strengthen us with might through Your Spirit within us. Dwell in our hearts to help us comprehend the love of Christ, remain rooted and grounded in love, and be filled with Your fullness. I know You are able to do abundantly above all that we ask or think according to the power that works in us. Help us access this power and operate in it for Your glory. Help us to recognize everything You've given us to fulfill our purpose. I ask You to send saints to encourage us as You develop and perfect the gifts You placed in us. I decree we will not get distracted with worldly things. Right now I separate us from corrupting influences and I decree we are vessels set apart for Your honorable and noble purposes. Father, I pray You count us worthy of our calling and purpose so all of our works of faith will be successfully completed. Thank You for preparing us to walk in the custom-made shoes You predestined us to walk in. Thank You for revealing Your calling for our lives and leading us into it. Though this world will pass away, I decree that we will abide forever because we live in Your will and carry out Your purposes. Thank You for giving us everlasting purpose. I am in agreement with these women of God and I believe what we've asked for is done in the name of Jesus, Amen.

Confessions

My husband and I cleanse ourselves from everything unclean. We separate ourselves from contact with contaminating and corrupting influences. We are a vessel set apart and useful for honorable and noble purposes. We are consecrated and profitable to the Master. We are fit and ready for every good work. (2 Timothy 2:21)

God gives us the spirit of wisdom and revelation in the knowledge of Him. The eyes of our understanding are enlightened to know the hope of His calling and the riches of His glorious inheritance in the saints. By this we know the exceeding greatness of His power toward us who believe according to the working of His mighty power. (Ephesians 1:17-19)

God saved us. He called us with a holy calling according to His own purpose and grace which was given to us in Christ Jesus before time began. (2 Timothy 1:9)

We are able to do nothing of ourselves but only as we are taught by God and as we receive His orders. Even as we hear, we do not seek or consult our own will. We have no desire to do what is pleasing to us or our own purposes, but only the will and pleasure of the Father who sent us. (John 5:30)

Day 23 Adversity

Father God, I come to You, in the name of Jesus, to ask You to train my husband and I to effectively respond to adversity. Only You know the internal and external distress we face in this world. I ask for instruction and grace to handle the distress in a manner that will bring glory to You. You taught that we should not be amazed at the fiery ordeal taking place to test our quality, but we should rejoice that Your glory will be revealed and we will be filled with exceeding joy. Lord, I ask for deeper understanding of how these trials come to perfect and polish us. I know that You are transforming us into Your image and this requires pruning and refining. Help us recognize the opportunity for growth and rejoice knowing that the trying of our faith works patience and maturity. Help us allow patience to do a thorough and perfect work so that we lack in nothing. I know in the world we have tribulation, trials, and distress but we are to be of good cheer because You have overcome the world and deprived it of its power to harm us. Father, condition us to approach adversity with this in mind so we will not be apprehensive or intimidated. I confess and repent for pitying myself and complaining in the past. When compared to the trials that our Savior encountered, I recognize that my trials are very small. Christ faced adversity to the point that His blood was shed. Lord, help us to remember this when we're tempted to feel exhausted, lose heart, or faint in the face of adversity. I declare, from this day forward, my husband and I will shake off the unnecessary weight that attempts to distract and entangle us. We will run the race that is set before us. You've ordered our steps, directed our path, and provided an easy yoke and a light burden. Condition us to stay on course and trust in You as our way-maker. I decree we will keep our eyes on Jesus, the author and finisher of our faith. I commit to encourage my husband and be patient with him so I will not add to the distress of his trials. Help me remember that the best way to help him is to intercede in prayer and trust You to work in his life. I know that those who wait upon You will renew their strength, mount up with wings like eagles, run and not be weary, and walk without fainting. Lord, I commit to wait on You. I will call out to You and listen for You to show me the way to go. I believe You cause all things to work together for good for us because we love You and we are called according to Your purpose. Thank You for making adversity, trials, and all other things work together for good. Thank You for allowing them to purify us and grow us closer to the image of Jesus. You are our refuge and our deliverer. Thank You for giving us Your peace. I am in agreement with these women of God and I believe we have received what we've asked for in the name of Jesus, Amen.

Confessions

My husband and I have perfect peace and confidence in God. In spite of tribulation, trials, distress, and frustration in this world, we are of good cheer because God has overcome this world and deprived it of the power to harm us. (John 16:33)

My husband and I know that the trying of our faith works patience. We let patience have her perfect work in us so we may be perfect, complete, and wanting nothing. (James 1:3-4)

My husband and I lay aside every weight and sin which desires to easily beset us. With endurance we run the race set before us. We look to Jesus, the author and finisher of our faith. Who for the joy that was set before Him endured the cross, despising the shame, and is seated at the right hand of the throne of God. (Hebrews 12:1-2)

My husband and I are blessed because God disciplines and instructs us. He has given us power to remain calm in adversity knowing that our Father will neither cast us off nor abandon us as His heritage. (Psalm 94:12-14)

Day 24 Blessing the Husband

Father God, I come to You, in the name of Jesus, to intercede for my husband. I call my husband a mighty man of valor after Your heart. I pray for an increase of understanding in Your word and Your ways. Enlighten him so he may know the exceeding greatness of Your power. I decree he is strengthened in the inner man and You dwell in his heart to keep him rooted and grounded in love. Father, help him comprehend the dimensions of Your love, know the love of Christ, and receive the fullness of You. I ask for Your angels to surround him and minister to him daily. Send him godly friends to be an example and encourage him with Your word. Sharpen his vision to see himself as You see him. I declare as he sees Your great plans for him, he will understand his purpose and endure all things. Lord, train me to see him and love him the way You do. I pray he sees clearly and walks boldly knowing You have ordered his steps. Thank You for assigning Your angels to keep my husband safe at all times. Thank You for leading him away from danger and provoking him to stay on the path You set before him. I call forth a prosperous mind-set in my husband. Lord, train him to cast down words and ideas that exalt themselves against Your word. I ask You to provoke him daily to renew his mind and speak Your word over himself, his wife, and our marriage. Condition him to speak only those things which edify and build up. I ask You to comfort and assure him that You hear his prayers and You are working in his life. Train him to wait on You, trust Your timing, and not grow weary in well-doing. I call forth integrity, faithfulness, diligence, holiness, purity, understanding, love, joy, peace, patience, kindness, humility, gentleness, and wisdom into my husband's life. Lord, I decree he will acknowledge You as the source of increase in all these areas. I declare that everything he puts his hand to prospers and he has favor with all men. Father, train him to dwell with me according to knowledge and to love me as he loves himself. I decree my husband is blessed in the city, in the field, in his body, and in his relationships. He is blessed when he comes in and blessed when he leaves. I declare everyone who comes against him one way, will flee before him seven ways. He is established in holiness as he keeps Your commandments and walks in Your way. Father, I pray You open the heavens and give him rain in the right season. I decree he will always be the lender and never the borrower. He is the head and not the tail. He is above only and never beneath. Lord, thank You for Your anointing on him. Prepare me to receive him as the husband You created him to be. Help me be a blessing to him as his wife. Condition me to walk in agreement with him so I never hinder his walk with You. I pray You bless him, keep him, make Your face shine on him, be gracious to him, and give him Your peace. Thank You for being able, willing, and faithful to answer my prayers. I am in agreement with these women of God and I believe what we've asked for is done in the name of Jesus, Amen.

Confessions

My husband walks worthy of his calling with lowliness, meekness, and longsuffering. (Ephesians 4:1-2)

My husband is blessed and he is a blessing forever. God makes him exceedingly glad with the joy of His presence. (Psalm 21:6)

My husband is happy because he finds wisdom and gets understanding. (Proverbs 3:13)

My husband is blessed because he trusts in and puts his hope in the Lord. (Jeremiah 17:7)

My husband diligently listens to the voice of the Lord. God sets him on high because he observes His commands. All of God's blessings accompany him. (Deuteronomy 28:1-2)

Confess all the blessings in Deuteronomy 28:3-14

<u>Day 25 Parenting</u>

Father God, I come to You, in the name of Jesus, to pray for us to be the parents You desire us to be. I know the world and everything in it belongs to You, including the children You bless us with. I ask You to train us to be good stewards over Your children. I call forth a renewing in our minds that will prevent us from repeating any ungodly parenting techniques modeled to us in childhood. I destroy all generational curses and decree they are no longer part of our family lineage. Father, I dedicate my family to You and ask You to make it a vessel fit for Your use. I ask You to mature us in prayer, wisdom, understanding, and love. Help us raise our children in Your way with Your discipline, love, and guidance. Where there is existing disagreement, I ask You to enlighten us with Your word so we may come together on one accord. Help us teach our children how to pray and relate to You. Thank You for giving our children ears to hear Your voice, eyes to see Your way, and wisdom to follow Your leading. I decree they know and obey Your voice and they will not follow the voice of a stranger. Help us train them to be accountable to You, do all things for You, and seek their reward in You. Quicken us to speak words that build up and refrain from those that would tear down. Season our words with salt so they minister grace to our children and provoke them to live righteous and holy before You. Help us train them to honor us so they may have a long, blessed life. Lord, I ask for wisdom to set boundaries that are protective but not unrealistic. I ask for discernment regarding what to allow in our home through books, movies, music, and games. Help us teach them to guard their heart and keep their mind on You. Father, I declare Your word abides in them, watches over them, and guides them at all times. I ask You to open our eyes to every teachable moment. Help us wisely use the rod of discipline to drive any foolishness from

60

their heart. I bind all rebellion, pride, and foolishness. I call forth obedience, humility, and wisdom in their lives. I decree our children live upright before You and they maintain a pure heart and a clear conscience. When challenging situations arise, quicken us to pray for a solution that is solid, effective, and based on Your word. Train us to discipline consistently and promptly without provoking our children to anger. Help us recognize when You are dealing with them so we can help them understand and respond to You. Lord, I know our children have great purpose in Your kingdom. I ask You to reveal their individual gifts and callings early in life. Help us encourage their development and train them to operate in their gifts for Your glory. I know they are like arrows in our hands. We will raise them as mighty warriors for Your kingdom. Help us train them in Your way as we stand on Your promise that they won't depart from it when they grow older. Help us live a life of worship and integrity so our children will want to choose the God they see us serving and obeying. Lord, help them see Your word working in our marriage to show them how to build theirs in the future. I proclaim we will pass on a spiritual inheritance that brings glory to Your name. Father, help us find fulfillment and joy as parents while never losing sight of our purpose as stewards over Your children. I am in agreement with these women of God and I believe we have received what we've asked for in the name of Jesus, Amen.

Confessions

My husband and I raise our children in the fear and admonition of the Lord. (Ephesians 6:4)
We train our children in the way they should go and when they are old they will not depart from it. (Proverbs 22:6)
Our children are a heritage from the Lord. The fruit of my womb is blessed. (Psalm 127:3)
As arrows are in the hand of a mighty man, so are our children. (Psalm 127:4)

Day 26 Mercy

Father God, I come to You, in the name of Jesus, to pray for an increase of mercy in my marriage. I am so thankful that You are good and Your mercy endures forever. There is no God in heaven or earth like You. You have great mercy on those who love You, fear You, and walk with You whole-heartedly. Today I come boldly before Your throne of grace to obtain mercy. Lord, You know the deep love I have for my husband. I never want him to have negative or condemning thoughts about himself. Right now I confess and repent for every time I was impatient and unmerciful with him. Forgive me for the cruel and judgmental things I said and did. Thank You for forgiving me and releasing me from this behavior today. Lord, help us resist the urge to harshly correct each other. Quicken us to intercede in prayer and trust Your Holy Spirit to reveal sin, bring conviction, and usher in repentance. Condition us to speak the truth in love and show mercy towards each other instead of accusing, blaming, and judging. You taught that when we conceal sin we do not prosper, but when we confess sin and renounce it, we receive mercy. Lord, help us to clearly recognize any sin in our lives. Train us to quickly confess and repent so we may receive Your mercy, healing, and forgiveness. Thank You for Your faithfulness to forgive us and cleanse us from all unrighteousness. Father, help us to humble ourselves and walk humbly with You. I decree, from this day forward, my husband and I will keep mercy and truth in our hearts so we will find favor in Your sight. We are Your chosen people, holy and beloved, so we will clothe ourselves with tender mercies, kindness, humility, meekness, and patience. We will quickly forgive others just as You forgave us. Lord, I confidently stand on Your promise that as we follow righteousness and mercy, we will find life, righteousness, and honor. Thank You for multiplying mercy, peace, and love in my marriage. I boldly declare that Your goodness and mercy will follow us every day and we will dwell in Your house forever. I am in agreement with these women of God and I believe we have received what we've asked for in the name of Jesus, Amen.

Confessions

My husband and I are blessed and have mercy because we are merciful. (Matthew 5:7)

God has shown us what is good and what He requires. We will do justly, love mercy, and walk humbly with our God. (Micah 6:8)

Mercy, peace, and love are multiplied unto us because we are sanctified, called by God, and preserved by Jesus. (Jude 1:1-2)

Day 27 The Past

Father God, I come before You, in the name of Jesus, to ask You to help my husband and I let go of the past completely. I present myself as a living sacrifice to You. I ask You to consume away everything that is not pleasing to You. I desire for us to fully walk as the new creation You made us to be. Help us strip off our former nature and discard our old, un-renewed self that is so easily corrupted through lusts and delusional desires. Train us to constantly renew our minds with Your word and put on the new righteous and holy nature created in Your image. Help us clearly discern Your voice so we easily distinguish it from the voices of the past. Thank You for placing Your Holy Spirit in me to work and speak Your will for us. Right now I rebuke all the ungodly teachings and examples set by the influences of the past. I call those memories lies and I cast them down. I decree they can no longer confuse or manipulate our thinking. Father, I ask You to reveal any bitterness, unforgiveness, or resentment that we are harboring towards anyone in our past. Right now I forgive everyone who ever hurt us. I release them and us from the bondage that unforgiveness brings. Lord, I ask You to reveal any area where we have not put away our old self. I know You have set us free from that dead weight and it is Your will for us to let it go. From this point forward, I decree my husband and I are no longer comfortable with those old ways, habits, and thoughts. Neither in word nor in deed do we identify ourselves by those anymore. I tear down those strongholds. I decree we are released and forever separated from those deceptive ideas and all the memories, sorrow, pain, ignorance, and death that accompanied them. Father, we accept Your word and Your ideas concerning who we are. Thank You for wiping away every tear from our eyes and promising that there shall be no more death, nor sorrow, nor crying, nor pain because the former things have passed away. No matter what happened in the past or how far out in the wilderness we traveled, You have reconciled us to You. We no longer remember the former things nor consider the past because You have done a new thing in us. Thank You for setting us free from the past. Thank You for the future You've given us that is filled with hope. Thank You for giving us clean hearts and renewing a right spirit within us. I am in agreement with these women of God and I believe what we've asked for is done in the name of Jesus, Amen.

Confessions

My husband and I are in Christ so we are new creations. Old things have passed away and, behold, all things have become new. (2 Corinthians 5:17)

My husband and I do not remember the former things. We do not consider the things of old. God is doing a new thing in us. We perceive it and give heed to it. God will even make a way in the wilderness and rivers in the desert. (Isaiah 43:18-19)

My husband and I strip ourselves of our former nature which characterized our previous manner of life and became corrupted through lusts and delusional desires. We are constantly renewed in the spirit of our minds. We have a fresh mental and spiritual attitude. We put on the new righteous and holy nature created in God's image. (Ephesians 4:22-24)

Day 28 Joy

Father God, I come to You, in the name of Jesus, to pray for an increase of joy in my marriage. I know that You came so we may have life and enjoy it in overflowing abundance. My heart's desire is that we truly enjoy life with one another. Lord, fill us with laughter and songs of joy as we acknowledge the special and great things You've done in and for us. You have truly done awesome things in our marriage. I am overjoyed just thinking about it. We have so much to be thankful for. Thank You for my husband. Thank You for the man he is becoming. Lord, raise me up to be a joy to my husband. I know You desire me to reverence my husband and that includes enjoying his presence, his conversation, and his company. I ask for the fun and laughter between us to be increased. Help us to be playful without being foolish. I confess and repent for the sarcastic things I've jokingly said in the past that hurt his feelings. I forgive him for every joke and sarcastic remark he ever made that hurt me. From this point forward, I pray Your Holy Spirit guides us, even in our jokes, to keep us from dishonoring or insulting one another. Train us to never return insult with insult but on the contrary respond by blessing one another. You taught that whoever wants to enjoy life and see good days must keep their tongue free from evil and eagerly search for peace and harmony. I decree from this day forward, my husband and I pursue peace at all times. We speak Your word and we refrain from speaking anything evil. Thank You for the joy to come as a result of us obeying Your word. Father, I ask You to develop our conversation skills so we will be able to speak the right words at the right time to bring joy and laughter. Lord, reveal new ways for us to appreciate and enjoy one another. I ask You to show me creative ideas and new activities that we can enjoy together. I pray these experiences knit us closer together in love. Lord, thank You for inhabiting the praises of Your people and promising the fullness of joy in Your presence. Condition us to praise You continually and remain in Your presence. Quicken us to always make melody in our hearts by reciting psalms, hymns, and spiritual songs to praise You. In the name of Jesus, I ask You to strengthen my marriage today through an increase of Your joy. I receive it and thank You that our best days are ahead. I love You and give You all the glory. I am in agreement with these women of God and I believe what we've asked for is done in the name of Jesus, Amen.

Confessions

My husband and I enjoy life in abundance. (John 10:10)
God has blessed us to be a blessing forever. We are exceedingly glad with the joy of His presence. (Psalm 21:6)
Our mouths are filled with laughter and songs of joy because the Lord has done great things for us. We are glad! (Psalm 126:2-3)
My husband and I have joy by the answer of our mouth. We speak words in due season and they are good. (Proverbs 15:23)

Day 29 Our Future

Father God, I come before You, in the name of Jesus, to ask for a vision of our future. I know Your plans for us are good and will give us a future and a hope. I ask for the spirit of wisdom, revelation, and the knowledge of You to enlighten the eyes of our understanding so we will know the hope of Your calling and the riches of the glory of Your inheritance in the saints. Help us to know the exceeding greatness of Your power in us. The same mighty power that was in Christ when You raised Him from the dead and seated Him at Your right hand in heavenly places far above all principality, power, might, dominion, and every name that ever was or will be. Help us understand how You put all things under His feet and made Him the head over all things to the church, which is the fullness of Him. Lord, train us to see things from Your perspective so we are able make wise choices. I decree we will no longer depend on our own understanding but instead we will acknowledge You in everything and trust You to direct our path. I proclaim we will walk by faith in agreement with Your Holy Spirit. In the name of Jesus, I ask for a clear outlook of where we are and where You are taking us. As You reveal Your ultimate plan for our lives I ask You to also show us the little steps we will take to get there. Help us focus on the steps You've ordered for each day and know we are making progress towards the end prize. I ask You to wake us up early to seek You and Your plan for the day before we get into our daily tasks. Quicken us to study Your word and remain rooted and grounded in love so we will not be shaken. God, I ask You to plant us firmly in Your house and keep us fresh, flourishing, and bearing fruit well into old age. Help me think of my husband often and find ways to help him. Even when I am over-tasked, I pray You give me the time, motivation, and grace to selflessly help him. I know as I do this, it will help him walk into his future with You. I call forth Your will to be done in his life just as it is in heaven. I decree Your plans for him will come to pass without delay or hindrance. Thank You for showing me that I don't have to convince him or nag him to change. I cast my cares before Your throne. I surrender my will and I ask for Your will to be done. I place our future in Your hands. I acknowledge the good work You've begun in us and I am confident that You will perform it until the day Christ returns. Thank You Lord. I pray my lips never cease to praise You. You are worthy. You are the source of every good thing. I find safety in Your arms. Thank You for being my Father, my Lord, my Provider, my Healer, my Strong Tower, my Deliverer, my First Love, my Master, my Strength, my Victory, my Peace, my Savior, my Help, and my God. You're everything to me. Thank You for showing us where we are, where You want us to be, and how to get there. We will not be disobedient to the heavenly vision. I am in agreement with these women of God and I believe we have received what we've asked for in the name of Jesus, Amen.

Confessions

My husband and I are planted in the house of the Lord. We shall flourish in the courts of our God. We shall still bear fruit in old age. We will be fresh and flourishing to declare that our Lord is just. He is our rock and there is no unrighteousness in Him. (Psalm 92:13-15)

God knows His thoughts toward us. His thoughts are of peace and not evil, to give us an expected end. (Jeremiah 29:11)

My husband and I sow to the Spirit and we reap everlasting life. My husband and I will not lose heart or grow weary in doing right. In due time and at the appointed season we shall reap because we did not faint. We commit to do good to all people. We will be mindful to be a blessing, especially to those of the household of faith. (Galatians 6:8-10)

Day 30 Closing Prayer

Father God, I come to You, in the name of Jesus, to pray for my marriage to more accurately reflect Your love. I ask You to reveal anything that is hindering us from being true ambassadors for Christ. I remove those things right now. I decree my conscience is purged from dead works so I may serve You. I ask You to mold my family into a godly example that inspires others to seek You. Lord, I see people searching for something to keep their family from falling apart. I see them giving up and splitting up because they don't know what to do. Lord, work through us to show them that You are the answer and nothing is impossible for You. You can restore the most-broken person and the most-broken family. Thank You for not giving up on us when we wanted to give up. Even then You knew the plan You had for us. Thank You for Your mercy and how You caused everything to work together for good. My family is now a living testimony of Your power and glory. We will never take that for granted or forget how far You've brought us. I lift up the families that are at the breaking point right now. I ask You to send laborers to minister Your love and power. I pray for those that don't know You and don't realize that everything they long for is in You. Work through me as a vessel to reach them. I cast down the lie that my family has to be perfect before I can help others. I stand on the truth that Your word is transforming my family each day and this will provoke others to seek and surrender to You. In the name of Jesus, I come against the adversary and all his attacks on families and marriages. I bind the spirit of confusion, the lying spirit, the spirit of bondage, the spirit of fear, the spirit of jealousy, the spirit of whoredoms, the spirit of pride, the spirit of heaviness, the familiar spirit, the spirit of divination, the spirit of infirmity, the seducing spirit, the deaf and dumb spirit, the spirit of error, the spirit of perversion, the spirit of the antichrist, and all other spirits sent by the enemy to steal, kill, and destroy. I command these spirits to evacuate the premises of all families. I call forth the light of God to expose every attack, trap, device, strategy, and stronghold of wickedness. I remove all blinders placed by the enemy. I declare, from now on, all family members will see sin for the disgusting thing that it is and they will renounce sin forever. I plead the blood of Jesus over all families and marriages. I decree the devil has no more place, foothold, entrance, or opportunity to operate. I call forth the spirit of holiness, love, power, truth, a sound mind, life, and adoption to abide in all families and marriages. I call upon every husband and wife to put on the whole armor of God and stand against the wiles of the devil. I speak to their ears and eyes and command them to open to God. Father, I pray for divine appointments to minister and disciple others. Thank You for choosing us to lead them to You. Thank You for allowing us to plant and water seeds for Your glory. I am confident You have begun a good work in my marriage and family and You will perform it until the day Jesus returns for us. I will continue to pray and worship You all the days of my life. I am in agreement with these women of God and I believe we have received what we've asked for in the name of Jesus, Amen.

Confessions

God commanded us to love one another. Just as He loves us, my husband and I love one another. By this people know that we are His disciples.   (John 13:34-35)
As my husband and I follow the example of Christ, others will follow. (1 Corinthians 11:1)
My husband and I let our light so shine before others. As they see our moral excellence and good deeds, they will recognize, honor, praise, and glorify our Father in heaven. (Matthew 5:16)

Testimonies

"In the past month I've seen my relationship with my wonderful husband just get better. We've always been the type to sit around and goof off and laugh and enjoy each other's company. We would be content to just stare at each other in the face (just as long as we were together)...but let me tell you...I feel so much closer to him spiritually now (not just emotionally and physically). Praying the prayers everyday made me realize what I needed to be praying for in my marriage...I thank God for each and every one of the awesome women of God who have come in agreement to pray for all of our marriages. I pray that your relationship with your Man of God is just as fulfilling. God Bless you all and I love you."
-Stace

"I want you to know my marriage deepened tremendously in the first 15 days of prayer. Now I'm continuing to pray daily and I'm seeing more and more growth. I can do nothing on my own, but I can do all things through Christ who strengthens me!"
-Nadine

"I thought my husband was reading the prayers because things were getting better and I thought he was making it happen. But he promised he wasn't and I realized that it is God doing it! I'm so happy."
-Amanda

"I am having the most amazing financial stuff happening in my business and I know it is because of the prayers and the effect they are having on our lives. God is good. I am grateful!!!!!!"
-Theresa

Testimonies

(From a husband to his wife)
"You must have read my mind; you just don't know how much more secure you've made me feel as a husband and father. I really have seen God grow in you and it makes me a better man! I have read some of the prayers you pray for me and it helps me work on that very thing you prayed for. I know that God gives me peace, but in the natural, you are just giving me the family of a lifetime. I want to be the perfect husband. I've seen your patience, love, and forgiveness grow by leaps and bounds and I have asked God to give me that same kind of love, patience, and forgiveness. I am in total agreement with what you say spiritually. I once thought it was all about the physical and natural, but now that we have the spiritual...I am so satisfied above measure. God has definitely placed me where I need to be with our family. I love you and God bless you woman of God."
-Jerome

"Thank you for this prayer. I got a chance to exercise mercy last night with my husband. I am learning that he does not think like me and some things he just does not know. I was using that as an excuse to be resentful and angry with him when he did not clean up or help around the house like we agreed on. God has given me a new heart and helped me to pray for him and help him in the areas that he is weak instead of making him feel bad. I love my hubby and I want to live in a peaceful home with a healthy marriage. Now I know what to pray and how to pray. I already see changes in me and the hubby and we have started to talk more and spend time with each other. It has also helped me not go off on him when he is not doing what I think he should be doing!!!"
-Carmen

Made in the USA
San Bernardino, CA
05 June 2013